Children of ISRAEL

THE WORLD'S CHILDREN

Children of
ISRAEL

written and photographed by
LAURIE M. GROSSMAN

Carolrhoda Books, Inc./Minneapolis

For Mom

Text and photographs copyright © 2001 by Laurie M. Grossman
Additional photographs on p. 19 courtesy of Independent Picture
Service. Map on p. 9 courtesy of Tim Seeley.

Carolrhoda Books, Inc.
A division of Lerner Publishing Group
241 First Avenue North
Minneapolis, MN 55401 U.S.A.

Website address: www.lernerbooks.com

LIBRARY OF CONGRESS CATALOGING-IN-PUBLICATION DATA

Grossman, Laurie M.
    Children of Israel / written and photographed by Laurie M.
Grossman.
        p. cm. — (The world's children)
    Includes index.
    Summary: Introduces the history, geography, and culture of Israel
through the daily lives of children who live there.
    ISBN 1-57505-448-5
    1. Israel—Juvenile literature. 2. Israel—Pictorial works—Juvenile
literature. [1. Israel—Social life and customs.] I. Title. II. Series:
World's Children (Minneapolis, Minn.)
DS118 .G8856   2001
956.9405'4—dc21   99-050907

Manufactured in the United States of America
1 2 3 4 5 6 – JR – 06 05 04 03 02 01

An Israeli boy holds his country's flag during a parade in the city of Jerusalem. The white and blue colors of the flag are the colors of the Jewish prayer shawl. The six-pointed Star of David in the middle is a traditional Jewish symbol.

Israel is such a small country that it takes just eight hours to drive its entire length. At its widest part, a drive across would take just two hours.

Located in the heart of the Middle East, Israel is a land of great contrasts. Visitors to Israel could cross mountain peaks, hilly green farmland, a sandy coastal plain, and a vast desert all in the same day.

More than six million people live in Israel. Of these, 80 percent are Jews, 15 percent are Muslim Arabs, and the rest are members of Christian and other religions. Hebrew and Arabic are Israel's official languages. Jews first settled the region around 2000 B.C. By 961 B.C., Israel was a unified kingdom. Beginning in 722 B.C., powerful ancient peoples such as the Romans conquered the land.

The Romans forced the Jews to leave the land and renamed it Palestine. These Jews fled to countries around the world. Some of these countries accepted the Jews, but others treated them poorly. Many Jews hoped and prayed for the chance to return to the land of their ancestors.

After the Romans exiled the Jews, people continued to live in and to conquer Palestine. From the 1500s, the land was ruled by Ottoman Turks. Arab farmers and shepherds, and a tiny Jewish community, were living there then. In the late 1800s, thousands of Jews fled attacks in eastern Europe and came to Palestine.

More and more Jews in Europe wanted to return to the place they called their homeland. But the Arabs living there did not want the Jews to come back. Throughout the early 1900s, thousands of Jews moved to Palestine. Soon after World War I (1914–1918), Britain was given control of the land.

In the early 1930s, Adolf Hitler and the Nazi Party rose to power in Germany. They planned to kill Jews across the world. By the end of World War II (1939–1945), more than six million European Jews had been murdered in what came to be known as the Holocaust. Jews everywhere began calling for a safe homeland.

Meanwhile, the Jewish pioneers living in Palestine were working hard to rebuild their ancient home. In 1947 Palestine was divided into a Jewish state and an Arab state. Arabs living in Palestine and in neighboring Arab countries did not want a Jewish state to form.

Above: *These columns in northern Israel were built by the Romans in ancient times.* Right: *The walls surrounding the Old City of Jerusalem were built hundreds of years ago by the Ottoman Turks.*

West Jerusalem is a mix of old and new neighborhoods. The area pictured below is more than 100 years old. Other, newer neighborhoods have been built throughout West Jerusalem since Israel's independence.

In 1948 the British left the land, and the Jews declared Israel to be a new independent country. Thousands of Jews returned to the home of their ancestors.

In the next decades, Israel and its Arab neighbors fought several wars over Israel's right to exist. In the wars, Israel won control of portions of neighboring Arab countries and of the Arab state that had been created in 1947. Many Palestinian Arabs moved to other Middle Eastern countries, but some continued to live in Israel and became Israeli citizens. Others stayed in the Israeli-controlled areas.

Conflicts between Israeli Jews and Palestinian Arabs have often turned violent. Palestinians have fought with Israeli Jews to have a place of their own to live. Many Palestinians and Jews have been killed by gunfire, and many Jews have been killed by bombs. Children learn not to touch lost bags, in case they contain bombs. The Israeli army patrols Israel and Israeli-controlled areas.

Some progress toward peace between Israeli Jews and Arabs has been made, however. In 1993 Israel signed an agreement with the Palestinians living in Israeli-controlled areas to work toward ending their conflicts. Israel withdrew from parts of this land to create a place where the Palestinians can live under a Palestinian-run government. Discussions about the right of Palestinians to Israeli-controlled land are ongoing. Since the late 1970s, the Israeli government has signed peace treaties with some neighboring Arab countries.

Even though peace agreements have been made, Arabs and Israelis continue to disagree and sometimes fight over the land.

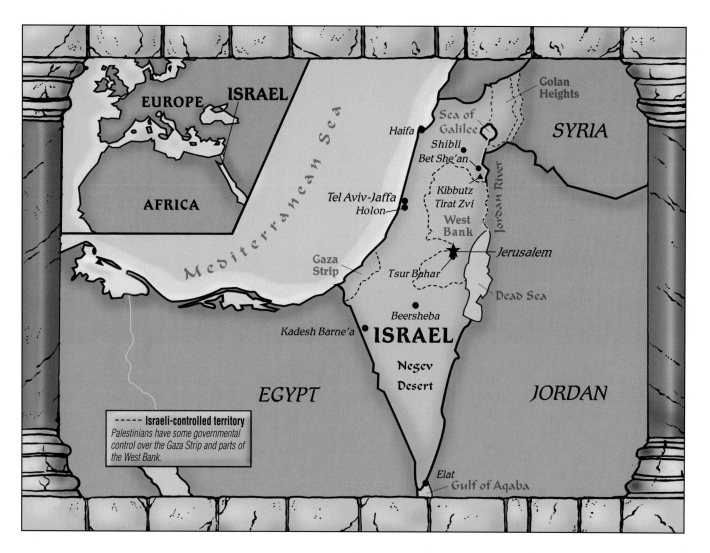

- - - - - **Israeli-controlled territory**
Palestinians have some governmental control over the Gaza Strip and parts of the West Bank.

Tel Aviv-Jaffa

Most Israelis live in big cities in the northern half of Israel, crowded into apartment buildings. One-fifth of all Israelis live in and around Tel Aviv, Israel's business center. (Tel-Aviv and the ancient city Jaffa have been connected since 1950, making the area's official name Tel Aviv-Jaffa.) Ori lives in the city of Holon, at the southern edge of Tel Aviv. His mother teaches computer classes, and his father delivers packages to businesses.

Ori wears his apartment key around his neck, so he can let himself in after school. His mother checks the notebooks Ori carries to first grade. She likes to see how well he is doing. Israeli children go to school six days a week. Jewish children and Muslim children attend separate schools.

Jewish children do not have school on Saturday, their holy day. The Muslim holy day is Friday. Muslims have that day off from school.

Ori's school is a typical Jewish Israeli school. Ori learns about reading, math, social studies, drawing, holidays, and science. Classes are taught in Hebrew. Like all Israeli children, Ori will start learning English in third grade.

Ori in front of his apartment building

Ori and his mother walk to the bus stop.

11

Ori and his grandfather Leon

Leon, Ori's grandfather, likes to walk Ori home from school. Leon is the only member of his original family who made aliyah, or moved to Israel. He considers himself very lucky. When Leon was a teenager in Poland, World War II broke out. The Nazis began forcing Jews into concentration camps, where conditions were horrible. Most Jews in the camps were worked or starved to death, or they were murdered. The Nazis killed four of Leon's five brothers and both of his sisters.

After the war, Leon remained in Poland and tried to help other Polish Jews learn Hebrew and move to Israel. For this, he was sent to a Russian prison in Siberia for 10 years. Life there was very difficult.

Leon had to work hard in freezing weather. He tried to make the best of the situation and was lucky to survive. Thousands of Holocaust survivors and Jews who were kept in Russian prisons came to live in Israel. Leon arrived in 1955, when Holon was mostly sand dunes.

Jewish refugees continue to arrive in Israel. Leon is glad his grandson is growing up free in Israel.

At Yad Va'Shem, the Holocaust memorial museum in Jerusalem, six stone blocks represent the six million Jews who were killed in the Holocaust. The Star of David in the middle, the traditional Jewish symbol, reminds visitors of the stars Jews were forced to pin on their shirts during World War II.

Yoni lives in Bet She'an. Temperatures here often reach 100 degrees. Most of the people who live in Bet She'an are Sephardic Jews. Most Israeli Jews belong to one of two ethnic groups. Sephardic Jews come from Spanish, North African, and Middle Eastern backgrounds. Ashkenazic Jews are of northern or eastern European descent, like Ori's family. The common thread that ties all Jews together is that their ancestors lived in ancient Israel and practiced the Jewish religion.

Yoni, his brother, and his mother stand in the entranceway to the sukkah, or hut, they built. Jews build sukkot and sleep and eat in them for a week to celebrate the fall holiday Sukkot.

Yoni's mother brings food back from the outdoor market in Bet She'an.

Yoni's brother decorates the sukkah. He dragged a dozen palm fronds from his grandmother's yard to build the hut's walls.

Yoni's grandparents moved to Israel from Iran in the 1950s. They raised 14 children in the house across the footpath from Yoni's house. Yoni's family feasts on foods like rice with herbs and spices. These are the same foods that their ancestors ate in Iran. Yoni's favorite is *hom-homs*, which means "hot-hot." This is fried dough dipped in honey. During hot summer nights, Yoni and some of his eight brothers and sisters sleep on mattresses on the cool tile floor.

Bet She'an is surrounded by rich agricultural land. For thousands of years, nations have fought for control of the fertile region around the city. From 63 B.C. to the A.D. 300s, Israel was part of the Roman Empire. The Romans built grand buildings and palm-shaded avenues in Bet She'an. They used the city as a capital to rule cities in Jordan and Syria.

Next to Yoni's house, ruins of the Roman city have been uncovered to create a vast archaeological park. There are bathhouses, bridges, and a theater, where Yoni and his friends play hide-and-seek.

The Roman ruins next to Yoni's house. The hill in the background contains ruins from many ancient cultures that occupied the region. Inset: *Yoni peers out from a hidden staircase in a Roman theater.*

Like many Israeli children, Yoni has a short break during school for *aruhat eser,* the ten o'clock morning snack. Children bring fresh bread rolls with chocolate spread or cucumbers, tomatoes, and soft white cheese. They drink *shoko,* a plastic sack of chocolate milk, which they tear open with their teeth and slurp. Other popular snacks for Israeli children are breaded chicken or soy patties with ketchup, fruit-flavored cheese puddings, and peanut-flavored corn puffs.

Yoni digs for aksus, *a root that tastes like licorice.*

17

Below: *Kibbutz Tirat Zvi's fishponds. The sharp mountain peaks are part of the country of Jordan. About 630 people live at Tirat Zvi.* Right: *Yossi at work as the kibbutz carpenter*

South of Bet She'an, a factory in Tirat Zvi makes another food that Israelis enjoy: hot dogs. Tirat Zvi is a kibbutz, which is Hebrew for "a gathering." A kibbutz is a shared settlement. The residents of a kibbutz work in the gardens, factories, day-care center, and in kibbutz-owned businesses, such as hotels. Traditionally, members of a kibbutz are not paid in money. Instead, the kibbutz provides them with what they need—food, clothing, and housing, as well as vacations and money for university education. Kibbutz children attend schools run by their kibbutz or one nearby.

Yossi works as the kibbutz carpenter. When Yossi got married, the kibbutz paid for his wedding and gave him a house. Instead of each family having its own car, the kibbutz buys several. Families use a car whenever they need it. They check it out, much like they check a book out of a library.

Kibbutzniks, as the residents are called, eat meals together in a big dining hall. They take turns cleaning up. If they feel like eating at home, they wheel carts with dinner back to their houses. They take the dirty dishes back to the community dishwashing machine when they are finished.

Above: *A kibbutz cafeteria.* Left: *A kibbutznik loads the cafeteria's dishwashing machine.*

19

Most kibbutzim have children's houses. There, children are grouped by age and spend a lot of time with others in their age group. Yossi grew up on a kibbutz in the 1960s. At that time, all the children slept in the children's house. These days, children sleep in their parents' homes.

Avishag and Esther are Yossi's youngest daughters. They like to pick pomegranates and pomelos off trees in their front yard. They learn about fruit trees from their grandfather, who rides an electric crane each morning to pick dates for the kibbutz.

Avishag and Esther's grandfather picks dates from one of the many palm trees on the kibbutz. The dates are wrapped in netted bags while they ripen on the trees. This way they won't fall off the trees and rot on the ground.

Left: *Esther picks pomegranates off the trees in her front yard.*
Below: *Avishag with her older sister, Tehila, who is visiting the kibbutz from her army training session. She is wearing her army uniform.*

Their older sister, Tehila, just started army training camp. Israeli boys are required to serve three years in the army when they finish high school. Unmarried girls serve nearly two years. Arabs are not required to serve. Some Jews do not serve for legal or health reasons. Some extremely religious Jews study in a religious school instead of serving in the army.

Above: *Ayman's town, Shibli, at the foot of Mount Tabor.* Right: *Ayman holds his baby sister.*

Ayman is a Bedouin teenager. Ayman and the residents of his town, Shibli, are Muslim Arabs. At home, Ayman and his family speak both Arabic and Hebrew.

Many Bedouin are nomads, which means they move from place to place. Bedouin who live in the desert move long distances to find water and pasture for their cows and sheep. But the residents of Shibli have settled permanently at the base of Mount Tabor. Ayman's tribe has lived at the foot of the mountain for 400 years.

The people of Shibli used to graze sheep, raise fields of sesame and wheat, and live in tents. These days, most Bedouin in Shibli work in offices, in factories, or on large farms outside the town. Ayman's father, the mayor of Shibli, started a business teaching people how to drive. Since the 1950s, the Bedouin in Shibli have built many concrete homes and a large mosque, or place for Muslim worship.

Right: *The sheik, or chief, of Shibli grinds coffee. All 3,000 people in the town have the same family name, Shibli.*
Below: *Himad Shibli is one of five boys in his class with the same name. His teacher is teaching him the word for* on *by having him stand on a chair.*

Haifa is Israel's biggest port city.

Haifa, a large city in northwest Israel, was built on mountains overlooking the bright blue waters of the Mediterranean Sea. The city is the center of the country's heavy industry. Factories in Haifa make steel, process oil, and assemble automobiles.

The biggest industry in Israel uses brainpower more than machines—it is research. Israel has a higher percentage of its workforce doing scientific research than any other country has. Basic natural resources, such as oil, coal, and water, are scarce in Israel, so scientists must work to find solutions. One-third of Israel's sales to other countries comes from technologies these scientists invent. Israeli inventions include tractors that are controlled by computers, lasers for use in surgery, and various programs for computers.

Near several computer companies on the Haifa coast is a trailer park, or *caravanim,* for new immigrants. In 1996, Tadela and his family came to Israel from Ethiopia, a country in Africa. Tadela's ancestors were among the Jews forced to leave Israel in ancient times.

Tadela loves doing handstands. He learned acrobatics from his teenage brother, Aychew. Aychew does gymnastics and juggles in a performance group of Ethiopian children.

Tadela at the caravanim *where he lives*

Tadela's grandmother makes *injara,* the main meal of the day. This spongy dough sits in the kitchen for a whole week before it is fried and served with meat or mashed beans. Each Saturday, Tadela's grandmother wraps herself in an embroidered white cotton cloth to celebrate Shabbat, the Jewish Sabbath, or holy day, just as she did in Ethiopia.

Above: *Tadela's 17-year-old aunt, Alemush, helps raise him.*
Right: *Alemush and Tadela's brother, Minevas*

Two-thirds of Jewish Israelis were born in Israel. The rest, like Tadela, immigrated from other countries. Many came to escape anti-Semitism, which means hostility toward or unfair treatment of Jews. They couldn't get the job, education, or home they wanted because they were Jewish.

The Israeli government helps immigrants by partially funding housing, transportation, and higher education.

Children from the caravanim *nursery school*

Anat lives in a different part of Haifa, in the hills that tower over the port below. She gathers with her youth group, B'nai Akiva, on Saturday afternoons. Most young Israelis belong to a youth group. Members of B'nai Akiva play games and win treats called *crembo*, chocolate-coated balls of cream and cookie. On summer nights, they gather for *kumsitz,* sing-along campfires, and they roast potatoes and onions in tinfoil.

Youth groups helped Israel become a thriving nation again. Beginning in the late 1800s, Jewish youth groups in Europe secretly met after school. They were part of the movement to return to the land of their ancestors. They studied Hebrew. Most of these Jews lived in cities. They had no experience in farming. So they studied farming skills to prepare for their settlement of Palestine. When they arrived in Palestine, they drained swamps, irrigated land, began farming, and started kibbutzim.

Above: *Anat and other members of* B'nai Akiva, *her youth group, painted this poster for a special weekend gathering. The poster reads "You and I will change the world." Right: Anat,* left, *and her B'nai Akiva counselor, Orit.*

Most modern-day Israelis work in cities, not on farms. Yet youth groups still do many things to help Israel and its people. Some help in hospitals or tutor immigrants. Anat's brother Menahem and other B'nai Akiva members from middle-class families spend twelfth grade volunteering in high schools in poorer communities.

For special celebrations, members of B'nai Akiva gather and march with torches and wave Israeli flags. For weeks beforehand, they prepare posters and signs about topics they discuss in their meetings. These topics include ecology, welcoming immigrants, settling Israel, and doing acts of kindness.

B'nai Akiva members carry Israeli flags as they march in a routine choreographed by the older counselors.

About two hours' drive south of Haifa is Jerusalem. The Old City of Jerusalem sits on the site of ancient Jerusalem, surrounded by a valley and a ring of higher peaks.

The Old City of Jerusalem contains sacred spots for three major world religions—Judaism, Islam, and Christianity. The Jewish holy place is the site of the Temple, last destroyed 2,000 years ago. Some Jews mourn the Temple's destruction in daily prayers. An outer wall of the Temple mount, called the Western Wall, still remains, and Jews pray there.

The Old City of Jerusalem

On the hill where the Jewish Temple once stood is a shiny gold dome called Dome of the Rock. This mosque marks the place where Muslims believe the prophet Mohammed rose to heaven. Thousands of Muslims come here to pray. To Christians, the Old City is important because this is where Jesus Christ spent some of his life teaching, and it is where he died.

Shmuel lives in the Old City. He plays soccer in stone courtyards, around columns that are more than 2,000 years old. In the Old City, archaeologists have found ancient baths, houses of worship, and utensils used by families at the time of the Temple. Shmuel's father, a judge, collects ancient oil lamps.

Shmuel on the porch of his house

Shmuel rides his bike down the narrow Old City alleyways, through ancient arches and marketplaces. Many Old City homes have domed roofs. Shmuel and his friends leap from roof to roof and scramble along walls that surround the Old City. About 450 years ago, Ottoman Turkish rulers built these walls with wide gates, towers, and narrow holes. The city's defenders used the holes for pouring scalding hot oil on their enemies.

Shmuel rides his bicycle down the narrow Old City streets. He and his friends often play soccer in stone courtyards.

One-third of Israelis, including Shmuel's family, practice one of several forms of Orthodox Judaism. Jews in Israel practice religious customs to different degrees. Some rarely go to a synagogue, a Jewish place of worship. They might or might not celebrate Jewish holidays and ceremonies. Some, like Shmuel, follow traditional customs and commandments from the Torah, the first five books of the Bible. They keep mitzvoth, the Biblical commandments about behavior, such as honoring one's parents and not working on Shabbat.

But some Orthodox Jews, including Shmuel and his family, also enjoy modern culture. They watch television and wear blue jeans. Shmuel has four older brothers, who have all served in the Israeli army.

Shmuel stands in front of an ornate synagogue door in the Old City.

Abba with his brothers, sisters, and cousins

Abba, in his family's kitchen, reads tales of legendary rabbis.

Abba lives in Jerusalem with his family, which includes eight brothers and sisters. Abba lives in a *haredi* neighborhood. *Haredi* means "fear" and refers to the awe the haredi have for God. Haredi Jews are ultra-orthodox. They try to have little contact with the modern lifestyle in Israel and concentrate on fulfilling commandments from the Torah. They do not own televisions or go to most movies.

Most families in the haredi community are large, like Abba's. Having children is considered a key mitzvah, one of the mitzvoth.

Haredi children attend a haredi school. They study Torah for most of each school day. They also study traditional school subjects such as reading and math. Haredi children attend school several more hours a day than other Israeli children. They have only a few weeks of vacation from school each year. Most 18-year-old haredi boys study Torah in a school called a yeshiva, rather than serve in the army.

Torah study is an important mitzvah in Abba's community. Families proudly display books that are devoted to Torah and explanations of it in their living room.

Many families in Abba's neighborhood run *gmaheem*. These are places that lend items that people need. When a family doesn't have money to buy diapers, toys, or furniture, they can get these items for free at gmaheem. They later replace them when they have enough money to do so.

Abba in front of his family's Torah library in their living room

Abba's favorite day is Shabbat. For religious Jews, this day is very different from other days. Many activities, such as driving and shopping, are forbidden. Instead, people devote the day to prayer, study, family, and rest. Abba enjoys retelling the deeds of great rabbis, or Jewish teachers and leaders, that he learns about at school. At home, families eat large Shabbat feasts. They invite guests to their home, including strangers.

In Abba's neighborhood, traffic is blocked off on Shabbat. Children play in the streets. Families walk to a synagogue and they visit friends.

Above: *A* haredi *boy at the Western Wall in Jerusalem. Thousands of people come here to pray and mourn the Temple's destruction.* Left: *Most Israeli children celebrate the joyous holiday Purim by dressing up in costumes. Purim celebrates a Jewish victory in ancient times.*

Haredi boys and their father at the Western Wall. Their father wears a fur hat like the ones his ancestors in Poland wore 200 years ago. Orthodox Jewish males grow out their sidelocks and wear a four-cornered garment with tsitsit, *knotted strings at each corner, under their shirts.*

Above: *Rawan.* Left: *Tsur Bahar, Rawan's hometown.* Lower left: *Rawan,* left, *her mother,* center, *and her sister, Ruba,* right. *The women cover their hair and Western clothing when they leave their home or when male guests visit.*

Rawan and her family are Muslim Arabs. They live in Tsur Bahar, a hilltop village of over 12,000 in south Jerusalem overlooking rolling beige hills. The cool mountain air in Tsur Bahar feels refreshing on summer evenings, when much of Israel is sweltering.

Tsur Bahar was built along the route of a stone pipe that carried water to ancient Jerusalem from springs 12 miles south. Israelis have always had to come up with creative ways to find water because it is so scarce.

Like most Israeli Arabs, Rawan and her family speak Arabic at home. Rawan dresses in traditional Arab clothes. She wears a long gown, known as a *jilbab,* over the pants and sweatshirts she wears at home. She has covered her hair since she was 12 years old.

Children in Tsur Bahar attend schools for Muslim children. They study religious subjects along with traditional school subjects. Rawan and her brothers attend separate schools for boys and girls. Her father, Mousa, is the principal of the boy's school.

The students in Rawan's brother Loay's class study math.

The courtyard at Rawan's school for religious Muslim girls. The girls are praying.

Tsur Bahar is made up of four large extended families, called *hamulot,* that have lived in the town for many generations. Respect for family is very important in traditional Arab culture. Girls help their mothers cook and clean as a sign of respect. Mousa's picture hangs in every room of his home. He is known as *Abu Nazir,* which means that he is the father of Nazir, his eldest son. Nazir is a successful construction contractor who built the finely decorated ceilings in his family's home. Mousa's teenage son Mohammed left school and works in construction. Mousa hopes that his youngest son, Loay, will study at a university as he did. Mousa's teenage daughter, Ruba, is training to be a teacher.

Mousa, Rawan's father, is principal of the Tsur Bahar boys' school. He teaches Loay's class Muslim mourning customs in the school courtyard.

During the month of Ramadan, Muslims fast all day. After sundown, they join together for a feast. Members of Rawan's *hamula* celebrate Ramadan together. They serve olives and lemons grown in the family courtyard. They feast on *mansaf,* or lamb, served with warm bread, known as *lahme.* This is usually accompanied by a heaping plate of rice with almonds, and *leben,* which is similar to yogurt. Everyone at the table shares and passes around plates piled high with food, rather than using individual dishes. Then, the adults move to a fancy sitting room, where they sip tiny cups of sweet coffee and enjoy honey pastries. Although Ramadan is a month of fasting, the family spends twice as much on food as it usually spends!

Rawan and her family enjoy the Ramadan feast.

The Makhtesh Ramon, or Ramon Crater, in the Negev Desert is the biggest crater in the world. Inset: *Visitors to the desert can take camels for a ride.*

Matan, Moriah, Oren, and Elinor live in the Negev Desert in southern Israel. They attend a high school dedicated to desert studies. In addition to the usual subjects, these ninth graders study maps, plants, features of the land and rocks, archaeology, first aid, and guiding others safely through the desert.

Though the Negev covers half of Israel's land, only 8 percent of Israelis live here. It is filled with rugged cliffs, canyons, vast craters, and sandstone in bright shades of red, violet, orange, and gold. Desert temperatures in August, Israel's hottest month, can exceed 125 degrees.

Matan, Moriah, Oren, and Elinor enjoy the wild desert beauty. Moriah finds the footprints of an ibex, a wild desert goat that scales sharp mountain cliffs. Matan spots an eagle soaring past and holes that snakes have burrowed. They go on hikes and sleep under the stars. They are careful never to litter.

Above: *Ibex, wild goats that can swiftly scale desert cliffs.* Left: *Oren.* Below: *These children sit near stone sculptures at the edge of the Ramon Crater.*

The Kadesh Barne'a community farm, where drip irrigation helps vegetables grow in the sand

A shopping mall in a desert town. Many towns in the Negev are modern like those in northern Israel.

Elinor lives in Kadesh Barne'a, a desert town on the Israeli-Egyptian border. Elinor's father conducts experiments growing plants in the sand. He has successfully raised artichokes, peaches, straw-berries, and other plants. He teaches Elinor about feeding plants the right amount of nutrients, even if none of what they need is found in the sand.

Elinor has a vast knowledge of the desert's treasures. She finds signs of life everywhere. A two-toed track shows that a deer visited, and another set of footprints belongs to a stork. She is able to identify many of the plants she sees. One plant is used to make rope, another plant is a mushroom she loves to cook with salt, and a third plant holds water in its roots.

For Elinor, the desert offers a peaceful way of life that takes her mind off news of troubles between Israel and its Arab neighbors. But she also remembers that her town sits on a border. Jews and Arabs have had so many years of conflict that all borders are carefully watched.

The residents of Kadesh Barne'a have practiced what to do in the event of an attack. Elinor hopes that Israelis and their neighbors will live in a calm balance, as the natural residents of the desert do.

Israeli children grow up facing several challenges. They will continue the struggle to make peace with neighboring countries that are often hostile. An equally great challenge will be living in a small country crowded with many different groups of people. But Israelis of all ages and religions have shown their ability to work together to improve their country. They continue to be hopeful for peace and a better future.

More about Israel

What kind of government does Israel have?

Israel is a democratic republic with a legislature, called the Knesset, that is made up of 120 members.

The prime minister is the head of Israel's government. Voters elect the prime minister. The president, who mostly performs ceremonial duties, is elected by the Knesset. Israel has many political parties. Usually two parties, the Labor and the Likud, are the dominant parties.

What kind of money do Israelis use?

The shekel. The shekel was used as a weight by the ancient Babylonians, Phoenicians, and Hebrews. The word *shekel* originally meant a unit of weight. The Hebrews first made coin shekels around A.D. 66.

What is the Dead Sea?

The Dead Sea is a body of water southeast of Jerusalem on the border of Israel and Jordan. It is called "dead" because it is so salty that plants and fish cannot live in it. People can easily float in its warm water.

Pronunciation Guide

Abu Nazir   AH-boo nah-ZEER
Bedouin   BEH-doh-ihn
Bet She'an   BAIT SHEE'ahn
B'nai Akiva   bih-NAY ah-KEY-vah
caravanim   kar-ih-VAH-neem
hamula   hah-MOO-lah
hamulot   hah-MOO-loht
haredi   hah-reh-DEE
Israel   YIS-rah-el (IZ-ree-uhl in the United States)
kibbutzim   kih-buh-TSEEM
kibbutz   kih-BUHTS
kibbutznik   kih-BUH-tsnik
kumsitz   KOOM-zeets
mitzvah   mits-VAH
mitzvoth   mits-VOHT
Muslim   MOOS-lihm
Ramadan   rah-mah-DAHN
Shabbat   shah-BOHT
sukkah   soo-KAH
synagogue   SIH-nah-gahg
Tirat Zvi   tih-RAHT TSVEE
Pronunciations given are as used in Israel.

Index